DIE HAPPILY

3 TRAITS TO LIVE A SATISFACTORY LIFE

RAVISHANKAR MURUGAN

Made with ♥ on the Notion Press Platform
www.notionpress.com

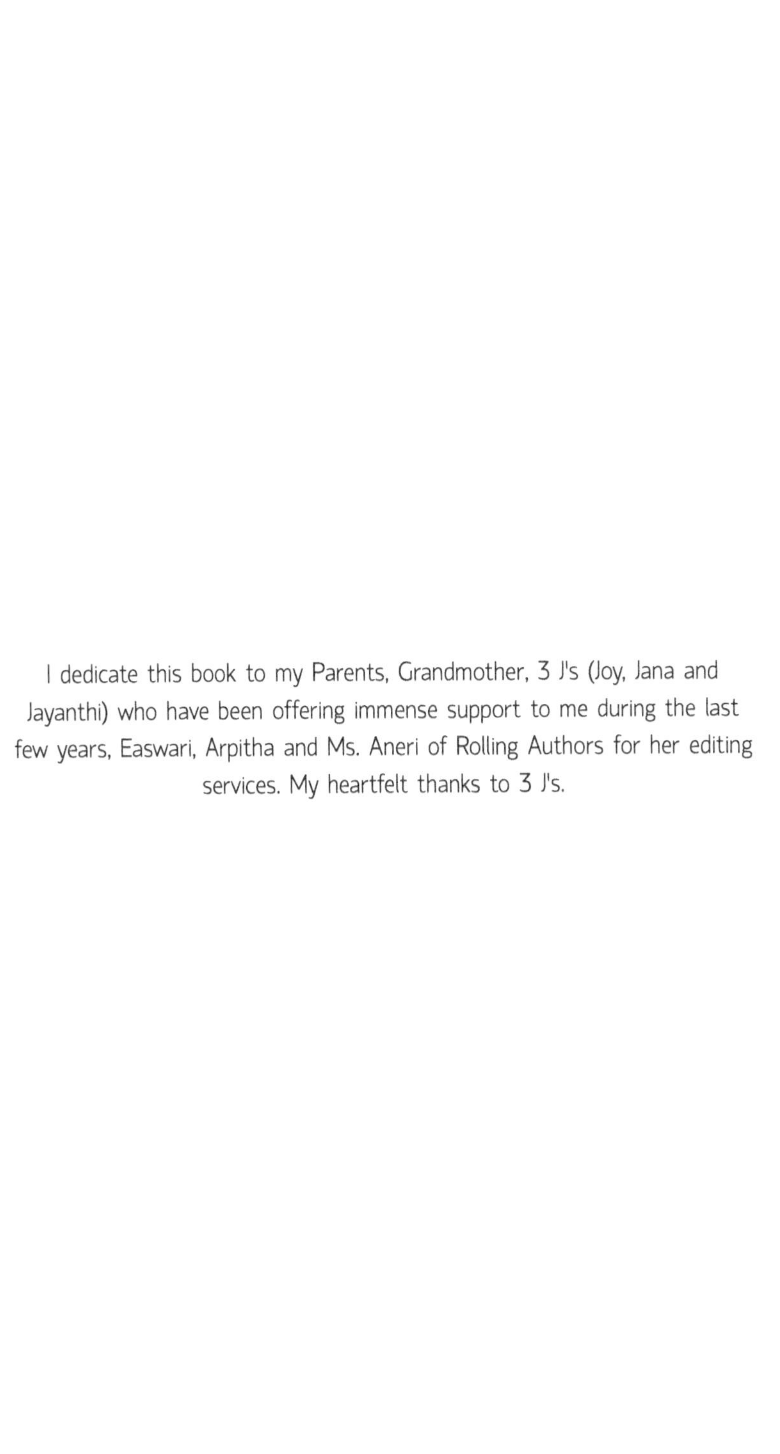

I dedicate this book to my Parents, Grandmother, 3 J's (Joy, Jana and Jayanthi) who have been offering immense support to me during the last few years, Easwari, Arpitha and Ms. Aneri of Rolling Authors for her editing services. My heartfelt thanks to 3 J's.

Contents

Disclaimer:

The information contained in this book is for general information purposes only. The author is not providing medical, legal, financial, or professional advice.

While every effort has been made to ensure the accuracy and completeness of the information, the author makes no representations or warranties of any kind, express or implied, about the accuracy, completeness, or suitability of the information for any particular purpose.

The reader should consult with a qualified professional before making any decisions based on the information contained in this book. The author shall not be liable for any damages or losses arising from the use of the information contained in this book.

The author has made every effort to obtain permission from copyright holders to reproduce images, tables and other materials in this book. Any omissions or errors are unintentional and will be corrected in future editions.

By reading this book, the reader acknowledges that they have read and understood this disclaimer and agree to hold harmless the author, publisher and their affiliates from any damages or losses arising from the use of the information contained in this book."

CHAPTER ONE

ARE YOU SURE YOU'RE ALIVE?

"I don't want to die!"

I looked up from the black screen of my phone that I held between my hands like an answer to some prayer that would magically make this situation all better. My friend was as limp as he was couple of weeks ago when he had been finally placed on the hospital bed after hours of multiple surgeries putting his body through the wringer.

I looked at the monitor, the beeping sounds coming from within were steady. Maybe I had just imagined those words.

But I hadn't. There it was again; mighty slow and raspy. But there alright: "I don't want to die. I haven't even lived yet."

I felt my sinuses clog up as I looked at the man I'd known all my life, unmoving on that stupid hospital bed. This wasn't fair.

'The bike accident has made him nothing more than a vegetable,' the doctor had said. Prayer was all he advised. The greatest scientific minds of our time, and faith was what he asked us to turn to when his surgeries only stitched my friend up but failed to make him better.

Times like these surely made one think. My friend had just been married. I had been there, at the wedding. Looking at the two of them from afar as they promised each other a life of happiness. There had been so much hope in their eyes.

Less than a few months later, my restless heart had found itself right here, in this chair, waiting for him to wake up.

It had been a few weeks since the day of the accident. But my heart seemed to be beating harder than ever today. Maybe I needed to let the worry out somehow.

I took one look at my friend again and the words rang in my ears, "I haven't even lived yet!"

I was almost sure I'd imagined them all on my own. Regardless, the words seemed to ring true. He had barely begun his life. If death was to come to take him today, or the next, or the day after, would my friend really be able to let go of life, certain he had lived it to the fullest?

There was no way I could know.

My hands shook anxiously as I looked around for something to pen my thoughts in. Maybe words would help me answer this very question for myself.

Death did that sometimes; put things in perspective. Maybe if I treated you—the reader—as I would treat my friend who lay on the hospital bed; maybe we could get an answer out for ourselves.

So, as I write this, I ask you the same question I ask myself, "Are you sure you're alive?"

Actually, I'm not the one that really needs an answer for this. Don't get me wrong, it's not like I'm asking you a rhetorical question. This is a question that deserves an answer by every person it is asked of. However, whether the answer is a 'Yes' or a 'No,' it reveals much about the person answering, both to the world and *to themselves*.

So, I ask you to ask yourself this time: Are you sure you're alive?

You can't really tell if you are? I have asked myself the same and it seems like I can't guarantee an answer either. Not yet, anyway. So, let's figure it out together by going back to the basics.

What do you think of death? I only ask you this so that I can share what I think it means to be alive. Let's try and define it together. In its most basic form, death seems to be a complete failure of body parts. After all, you are only alive as long as the essential organs in your body are running.

Sometimes, something inside us breaks. For whatever reason, an organ or two might go into failure. But that doesn't necessarily tell us it's a death sentence. We might replace the broken organ with a new functional one that could allow us to extend our lives. And by the technical definition of life that we just considered, it would mean that we've cheated death, and so, upon a literal technicality, are still alive.

So, does that mean we can live for hundreds of years? Or for at least as long as science can help keep our bodies running? Could it also mean that once our bodies are buried and decaying, we cease to exist completely?

Maybe.

But life isn't usually defined as simply as we have dared to define it here. To be human is to know that it's not just the efficient running of our bodies that answers the question of whether we're actually alive. Because by that definition, my friend was completely alive!

Let's consider the brain for example. Yes, it is an organ. And yes, when it fails, people will most definitely be considered dead.

So, technically, Mahatma Gandhi is dead. So is Mother Teresa, Nelson Mandela and Swami Vivekanand.

But still, we, as a race, seem to know of them very well. We take their teachings into our daily lives. Sometimes live by them like we would live by a law.

Why? They're dead. All traces of them should be gone. After all, their bodies are.

But the fact is the exact opposite, isn't it?

We equate almost every act of kindness shown on this planet to Mother Teresa's teachings. We learn quite early on in our lives, especially as Indians, that violence isn't the answer to everything, thanks to Mahatma Gandhi. We try to live our lives as impactfully as Nelson Mandela or Swami Vivekanand.

Why? Why would we follow dead men and women? These are people who should've stopped existing the moment their bodies were lowered into the ground, aren't they?

But the answer to the above question just leads me to one conclusion: our initial assumption of the definition of life must be wrong.

And it's put us back to square one. If we can't consider the day our bodies are gone as the day our existence ends, then what exactly is death; and by its extension, life?

Can it be what we leave behind? A legacy of some kind? If we were to follow the above example of some of the greatest people our generation, and the generations before, then yes, the answer would be their legacies. They would live forever as long as their teachings and philosophies remained within our ways of life and their names remained in our history books.

But then what of the common man? The one who didn't have his name written in history? What of the man who lived life to its fullest but didn't leave behind any legacy nearly as impactful as the names written above? Would he just die off only because our history textbooks didn't recognize his name? Would his life have no value to be considered then?

It can't be just a legacy that defines a life well-lived. Not for the majority of the population at the very least.

Let's assume for a quick minute that neither our physical bodies nor our legacies stay behind in the world. What happens then? How do we define life? How do we know that we're alive?

In the few decades of my life that I have lived, I have met more than a few people who have since passed on. For some, it was instantaneous. For others, it was a prolonged affair. And I'm hoping this wouldn't be the case for my friend on the hospital bed.

Regardless, after having talked to people who were dying, the general consensus seemed to be that there was always some sort of an acknowledgment of death right before they walked into the light.

I have heard of some studies that show that the brain is active for about seven minutes after the heart stops. So, the whole concept of 'life flashing before our eyes' right before we greet death might be at least half the truth. In which case, we might only find out just how well we've lived right before our deaths. But that is only if we overcome the fear of dying. And once that acceptance of death finally settles into our bones, we can finally look back on how we've lived and find an answer to whether we were really alive while our bodies were still functioning.

But, like quite a few others I know, I too hate the thought of having to wait till the very end of my life to figure out if it could be considered a well-lived life at all.

So, I will try and redefine what it means to be alive. While death and life can't help but coexist, almost like yin and yang; there is another, very important factor that helps define just how alive we were in our lifetimes: *Satisfaction.*

It's quite an elusive word, this—*satisfaction.* It seems to be quite different in how it's understood by many and how it's defined by some. Some may say, 'To be satisfied is to *have everything.*' Others may say, 'To be satisfied is to *want for nothing.*' So, just like the concepts of death and life, satisfaction is also dependent on the person defining it.

And yet, for ninety percent of the human population, satisfaction comes from owning much of everything presented by the world. This is why it's no surprise that people rarely find themselves satisfied with what they have or how they live. Because what they have is somehow never enough.

A car that was invented for the sole reason of taking you from one place to another, has now become a status symbol. And now, instead of just being a mode of travel, it defines the quality of life for its owners.

People stand in line for hours or wait in front of their computers with their eyes wide open every time Apple launches a new product just to spend their money on things they don't necessarily need. Big houses and even bigger egos seem to be the standard motivator behind human drive these days. The definition of a successful life, and a satisfactory life, has been contorted enough for most of us to think the only possible access to it is through even more money.

If only that was even half the truth. Though it is marketed to be the only truth these days.

Think of those monks and saints we've heard of at least once in our lives who guaranteed that they were living a truly satisfactory life after shedding the capitalist skin that the world is so proud about wearing themselves.

I'm not saying that completely letting go of a life of want is the only way to live a good, satisfactory life. If it was, I doubt the human race would've evolved much further than discovering fire. But it sure seems to be better than constantly wanting something we don't actually need to survive. It must be better than constantly second-guessing ourselves, our success, and our purpose by pitting ourselves against the person next to us who seems to own bigger and better things.

So then, if we can't live a satisfactory life by wanting things that we don't need, or by becoming someone like a monk or a saint, how then, are we supposed to live something even akin to a satisfactory life?

As I wondered about such secrets of life, I remembered something. Something stuck in the back of my mind. It was this unrelenting sound that reverberated through my skull until I managed to suck these words out: *respect, care* and *support.*

And I asked myself, 'Did I respect what I wanted to do in my life and put enough effort into it?' 'Did I give much care to it and to the people around me?' 'Did I offer enough support to myself when I needed it, and to other people around me when they did?'

It seemed to be quite a task I'd assigned to myself to sit and introspect about my life, or how well I'd managed to live it, when I didn't have an exact scale to measure it by.

I had come across death and accepted it as a single unchangeable fact of life, and still, it had put me no closer to the answer I had wanted to discover. I had considered the possibility to go against the norm and live my life like a monk, devoid of all wants and needs in order to say at the end of it all, I'd lived a satisfactory life. But it was all, after all, a path with no guarantee.

So, I sat with the words: *respect, care* and *support,* ringing in my ears until I figured out where to aim them at in order to get the result I so desired.

And then almost like magic, it clicked.

When you define something as good, most times the synonymous word used within a similar context is 'healthy.' Take relationships for example. Healthy relationships are good relationships. And they become so when both parties put in efforts to show their respect for each other, care about what the other wants and needs, and supports them through their ups and downs.

It occurred to me then that *health* was the missing parameter that would bring me a lot closer to my answer than ever before. In which case, it would do us well to take a look at our lives with focus on health.

So, how healthy have you been in your life?

And that is exactly what I asked my friend on the hospital bed, when he woke up after weeks of everyone around him being unsure if he ever would open his eyes again.

But, let me clarify that when I speak of health, it isn't just physical health I speak of. Physical health is but one of the six pillars I consider a must to master to reach the ultimate goal of a satisfactory life.

Let me introduce you to these six pillars that can measure and define a well-lived life, and not just one survived.

1. Physical Health
2. Mental Health
3. Financial Health
4. Intellectual Health
5. Social Health
6. Emotional Health.

This above list seems to be the least subjective way of figuring out whether we are actually alive, or just going through the motions of life as they come at us.

Now that you are made aware of these pillars that could define your life, we will surely discuss it further later on, and in as much detail as possible. But for now, since you have an initial scale to measure the quality of your life by, let's try an exercise together and see what it reveals to us about ourselves.

Put that phone you have been scrolling on for the past hour aside for a few minutes. Don't worry, this exercise will be much more helpful to you than whatever you were busy consuming on that device.

Have you done it? Great.

Now follow the instructions below:

Close your eyes for 15 minutes. Make sure you are not around anything that could potentially distract you within that time frame. After you've made sure of it, imagine that you are going to die within the next 3 minutes.

Once you have imagined it, and convinced your body of the same, ask yourself again: *Have I done everything I could to live a satisfactory life?*

CHAPTER TWO

THE CHASE OF PERFECTION

I found myself sitting again, but this time, not near a hospital bed. It was a lovely home. The dining room of which, unlike the dreadfully colourless room at the hospital, was smelling like flowers, some—fresh like the rain in the atmosphere, others—dying, like my friend had been on his hospital bed.

There was no incessant beeping of the machine that had kept my friend alive either. Although, my mind dearly wished for a way to point out signs of life again on an empty plot of land.

The chair I was on was comfortable, with wooden hand-holds and legs, carved with a pattern typical to older Indian households. It was the only thing left in the house that reminded me of traditional Indian designs. Everything else had been modernised and suited to the country that the owners of the house found themselves living in. A country I now found myself travelling to only to witness one more tragedy of life for myself.

I heard the keys rattle in the front door. Immediately, the silent sniffling that I heard soon after told me that the owners had just arrived home.

I stood up and straightened my shirt just as my friend walked into the dining room with her husband. Her eyes immediately began filling with more unshed tears—though, I wasn't sure how she could cry any more than she already had.

"You made it." She said, her voice completely devoid of any detectable emotion but sadness.

I didn't trust myself to reply. How could I? What could someone say in a situation like this anyway?

I looked at my friend's husband's face. There were a few new lines of white dotting his hairline. Though there were no tears, the sadness in his eyes was unmistakable. Even though words had deserted me, my body responded to this strong emotion just like anyone else would have.

I took a few rushed steps towards both of them and pulled them into a tight embrace. Hoping my tight grip would convey how heavy my heart was for their loss.

"I wish I had visited earlier. Under better circumstances." I whispered as soon as I let go of them, though it was quite apparent that my sincerity had barely been noticed over my host's emotions at the moment.

And just like that, the moment passed by in an instant and my friend was back into hostess mode, glad to have a distraction around to keep her away from the depressing reality.

"I know I told you to let yourself in but I hope you haven't been waiting for too long. I'll make you some tea." She said and immediately reached out towards one of the upper kitchen cupboards and pulled out a large mug.

"You don't need to tend to me right now," I said when I noticed that she had completely stopped in her tracks. Her gaze was fixed on the full-sized mug in the cupboard that had stood beside the one she had just pulled out to make me that incredible tea I had the privilege of having all my college years that I had spent at her family home.

"She loved this mug." My friend sniffled again. I could hear her take another deep breath in, trying to keep the dam shut on her sadness.

"It got her through quite the horrible times." This time, my friend smiled, and after another second or so, shut the cupboard door.

"Were you with her? When it happened?" I asked, silently kicking myself for risking a complete breakdown of my friends.

Surprisingly, no breakdown occurred.

My lovely friend only sat in a chair nearest to her, still holding the mug I was supposed to get my tea in, and smiled sadly.

"I was. I mean, we were. Honestly, it was just so sudden." My friend began.

That night, sitting in their guest room, I picked up the note book I had acquired for myself a few months ago in that hospital room. I had been diligent about noting down my thoughts about life and the satisfactory quality of it since the day I'd seen my friend slip into a coma. It had now become almost like a habit to break my thoughts down at the end of the day to see what new life lessons I'd learned and how much better I'd managed to live when compared to the previous day.

So, I began writing again. But this time, all I could think about and ponder upon was my friend's daughter. The same one who's bedroom was only two doors down the hall. A room that would never be the same again.

From what I remembered; she'd always been a brilliant child. Always first in her class. Always the kindest. Always the smartest within whatever group of people she was put in. She was one of those kids who at the mere age of ten had the mental capacity to ponder upon life and ask the kind of questions the universe still didn't have an answer to.

I still remember that one day when I had visited her family for the summer holidays. She must've been not much older than fourteen. We had been out in the sun, enjoying a quiet day with family and friends when she'd sat beside me with a little lily in her hand.

I couldn't seem to forget that face of hers even today. She'd looked up at me with wide eyes and a question burning on her tongue.

"What is it?" I'd asked; a smile playing on my lips appreciative of the inquisitive nature of the little girl.

"What do you think about success?" She'd asked and frowned. Her eyebrows had knitted themselves together to show her intense focus as she waited for some wise words to come out of my mouth.

I knew back then that girls usually matured faster than boys but I hadn't expected her to ask questions like that just yet.

I didn't even remember what my answer had been that day. I suppose it didn't matter in the end. Judging by the way things had turned out for her, it seemed like the adults around her had failed her.

I couldn't shake the memory of her so I started jotting down little details of her in my notebook. They were little snippets of her life but looking back at them, I thought they had been enough for me or any adult in their life to see the trajectory that her life was taking.

I wrote down what a typical day in her life as a medical student had been like. She'd been quite young when she'd been accepted to one of the top medical schools in this country. In fact, she must've been the youngest in her class, I think.

She would wake up quite early to prepare for her entrance exams and study for hours. Sometimes even till the sun was high up in the sky burning down on all of us. She would barely notice the food she put on her plate or in her stomach. Always quizzing herself with flashcards she'd never forget to bring to the dining table with her.

She'd barely give herself twenty minutes to gulp down her lunch and dinner and rush right back into her bedroom to pick up wherever she'd left off.

At the time, this behaviour didn't seem to any of us to be harmful in any way. All we saw was how ambitious the little girl had grown up to be. We saw the strict discipline she held herself to and bet on how quickly she'd find success because of those traits.

And find success she did.

She passed her entrance exams with top marks, was the youngest to be admitted in her class and was awarded a doctorate quicker than one could say, 'I can do that too!'

But her chase for success didn't end there. In fact, the more I got to know her as an adult, the more I understood that it wasn't success she was chasing after all. It was perfection. A quality the greatest minds of the universe tell us specifically not to fall for. Not in ourselves or anybody else.

I wish I'd told her this then: 'Perfection is nothing but a poison to what we perceive as satisfaction.'

Because it is. The concept sounds quite grand as we speak it;

PERFECTION.

But I have seen a great many people never finish a thing they'd started in the chase of perfection. And in the process, the chase would almost always eat them up.

Perfection is nothing but a lie. A fairytale concept to keep striving towards an endless goal.

And that is exactly what she'd done. She had given herself to the chase of it and in the process, forgot a very important thing for herself.

After she'd been awarded the doctorate and had begun practising medicine, she'd rarely pay attention to herself. Especially her body.

Soon, there hadn't been a day when she wouldn't need to take a pill to quieten that headache banging in her skull; or a pill she needed to help her sleep soundlessly; or a pill to fix the constant acid reflux in her chest.

In her chase for success, she had unconsciously ignored one of the most important things in life; one of the six defining pillars of the quality of life, which when maintained correctly, more often than not leads to a satisfactory life: PHYSICAL HEALTH.

Had she only given her physical health the same importance as she had given her intellectual well-being, maybe the outcome of this week wouldn't have been so very tragic. Maybe if she'd exercised when she'd needed to, slept longer and intensely instead of obsessing over being the greatest at everything, she would've enjoyed what she'd managed to achieve at such a young age.

Studies do show that exercise and taking care of your physical body releases endorphins. 'Endorphins are what makes you happy,' some people would claim. Regardless of it being the entire truth, taking care of the vessel that your soul and your mind reside in seemed to be an obvious thing to consider while mapping out a path to a well-lived life.

"Why didn't I tell her that then?" I wondered to myself as I wrote the same in my diary and circled it a few times in regret.

Had she shown the same amount of respect, care and effort to her body as she did to the growing knowledge in her mind, maybe today, I would be here celebrating her and her achievements along with her instead of wondering if the room two doors down the hall would ever perceive the slightest hint of happiness again.

Maybe the fault all lay with the adults by her side.

Suddenly, my mind flashed back to her question on the day of the picnic: "What do you think about success?"

And in complete terror, I heard myself echo someone else's words like a parrot: "Imagine it like the highest peak of the mountain. If you've climbed the great beast, reached the highest point, you've achieved success. Whatever it is in life that you want to do, imagine the highest honour it can bestow on someone, and then aim for that."

While you could say that was solid advice to give someone who merely sought the meaning of success, I feared I may have helped set her down a path of no return.

I should've added something to this definition back then. I should've said, "But remember, no amount of success, attainable or otherwise, is worth you."

I should've said, "Remember to always put you first."

I should've said, "Being truly happy and satisfied is how you can consider yourself successful."

But I didn't. I didn't say any of those words back then. And it was only because I didn't know of the truth back then myself. I only ever measured success the same way the greedy world did. I measured it with even more greed.

I closed my eyes and recalled all the degrees and certificates and trophies hanging on the walls two doors down. And then, imagined the white cloth over the deathly still body of my friend's daughter I had imagined when I'd first heard the news a few days ago. I was told that she had died of a heart attack. The doctors had informed her parents that had she exercised, and reduced the amounts of pills she took to keep walking on her path, she would not have died this young. Not of a heart attack at the very least.

I regretted not seeing the signs early, I regretted not knowing myself that how I defined a satisfied life back then wasn't the truth at all.

I let the two separate pictures fill my mind as I kept my eyes closed. One of my friend's, on the hospital bed in a coma, the other of another friend's daughter no more in this world and let myself realise how important this journey of mine had now become; the journey to figure out how exactly one can live a good and satisfied life.

For only one fact of life was an eternal truth: Death can always come for everybody, anytime. Our only real duty is to make sure we've given life a real chance and a true meaning when it does.

I shut my diary with a snap and took a deep breath as I wondered what else life had in store to teach me.

CHAPTER THREE

THE RIGHT KIND OF LOVE

A few years later, I found myself out of my home country and settled into a space that had previously been quite foreign to me except in thoughts connected to romance and love. That's right, I had been assigned to Paris for work. I was supposed to be in the country for about the length of two years and was expected to go back home as soon as all the deadlines for my project were met.

There had been a lot of adjustments. This wasn't the first time I had been assigned to a team in a different country but it definitely was my first time in France. I wasn't going to complain though. For most of my life, I'd proclaimed myself to be an avid lover of art in any form. And I was in a country where it was hailed to be the highest form of expression for the longest of times. How could I crib about being away from family for such a long time when I had access to such greatness just a single train ride away?

It had quite easily become a ritual of sorts for me to take that train every weekend and walk to one of the most famous art galleries in the world. I still remember the first time I'd walked through those doors. Being blinded by beauty wasn't exactly how I'd put it, but being fulfilled by perspective seemed to stick better when I tried to describe it to my friends back home.

One such visit of mine to the gallery introduced me to a young man I'd never seen there before. It was a quiet morning, just like every other weekend of mine. But the gallery, as always, was packed with people from all over the world. All come together to appreciate the art and pity the artist.

I say 'pity the artist' because according to the introduction cards below their works, most of them had met tragic ends in their lifetimes. Even if they lived centuries apart, it was like tragedy followed these people through time. It was a horrifying thought: "The price of true art is pain."

I refused to ponder on it anymore just in case I reached towards an agreeing conclusion. I didn't need that kind of negativity in my life right now. Or ever.

So, I tried not to read their introductions as I let my eyes pan over their beautiful works. I took in only what I could appreciate and discarded everything else.

And that one day, I found something else to appreciate. Something that hadn't been hanging in the art gallery before.

There he sat, the young man, on a bench near the gallery, with a sketchbook in his hands. He seemed to be ignoring the rest of the world just like it was paying no attention to him.

But the expression on his face was what had caught my attention initially. He seemed so focused, so attentive to his sketchbook....so greedy. Greed for what? At the time I could only guess it was for whatever he was sketching on those pages.

Days went by and as it were, I saw him on the same park bench every time I visited the gallery. Most times, holding the sketchbook and pencil in his hands, sitting with the same expression of him trying to constantly chase something that was always just out of his grasp.

It was when I saw him for the seventh time that I decided to walk over and strike up a conversation.

"Hey man, what's that?" I pointed at his sketchbook and sat next to him. He immediately shifted a little to the side, making space for me on the bench.

"Uh…nothing. Just something I've been trying to perfect." He tilted his sketchbook toward me so that I could have a better view of whatever he was working on.

It was a breathtaking replica of one of the works from inside the gallery. Although it was just a sketch and not truly painted out, the similarity could not be lost on me.

"This is beautiful!" I could not help but gasp out in awe. "You are truly talented, young man!"

A slight smile graced his face as he looked on at the sketchbook in his hand. Yet, the smile was anything but full of happiness. I wanted to ask right then if there was something wrong, but for some strange reason, I couldn't broach the topic with him just yet.

I let the thought fall back into my mind and moved on with my days. I had begun to add an additional task to my routine now. While I visited the gallery every weekend, I made sure to find the young man, always sitting on the same bench, and strike up a conversation with him.

As the weeks passed by, we became friends with our mutual love for art and a strange want for companionship.

On one of the most beautiful sunny days of the year, I finally decided it was time to really ask him what he was doing here.

"Why do you come here every weekend on the same day and practice the same work from the same artist?" I sat back on the bench, relaxing for what I hoped was going to be an enlightening conversation.

"Because she loves it." The young man said and bit his lip almost as if hesitating before deciding to reveal more about his motivations.

I waited patiently and let him sort out his thoughts before he could continue.

"There's this girl. I've loved her for as long as I can remember. And I thought…I think she loves me too." He continued while packing his bags, signalling he was done for the day. He leaned back on the bench just like I had and looked up at the clear, bright sky.

"I really do love her. But she…" He paused again so I turned to him and nudged him to continue.

"She thinks I'm too short." He spoke almost in a whisper, embarrassed more by the reason for her lack of love rather than the fact that he was indeed, short.

My face must've betrayed the ridiculousness I felt inside regarding the reason for his love not succeeding.

He took one look at me and sighed. "I know! It sounds like a stupid reason to not be with someone. But it seems to matter to her. And I love her. So, it matters to me."

"Then what are you doing here instead of trying to convince her that height is not really something to be worried about when it comes to love?" I asked and almost hit myself on the head. After all, wouldn't he have tried already? He was younger than me, but he wasn't too young to not have figured that out by now.

His expressions mirrored my thoughts immediately.

"Of course, I've tried! It just doesn't work! It's not enough for her! I'm…not enough for her." He said and I stayed silent this time just to give him space to really spell out what he'd been feeling for quite some time now. "That's why I come here you know. Every week. That's why I am trying to perfect this stupid painting. We met back in college when I was getting my art degree. I met her through a friend. She'd been introduced to me as the biggest art lover on the planet. I fell in love with her, asked her out, we dated for a while, but…

I thought if I became as good as her favourite artist, I might be finally enough for her to be with for the rest of her life. That's why I keep practising and trying to get as good as her favourite artist hanging in that gallery. Because when I do get as good as him, she'll finally be able to see beyond my short stature and look at what I bring to the table besides my love for her."

He was compensating for his height by trying to become a better artist in hopes that she'll love him again!

I wanted to say a few different things. Like: "Your love should've been enough." Or, "Your height shouldn't even be a problem if she really wanted to give you a chance." Or, "You deserve so much better than this."

But I didn't. I couldn't let any of those sentences out of my mouth after seeing that absolutely heartbroken expression on his face. Whether the girl loved him or not, I was certain this young man wanted nothing else in life but her.

In any other situation, this realisation would've filled my heart with a little bit of hope about the cruel world, but right now, it only added to the tragedy of it.

I decided this was enough for the day. So, I helped the young man calm down and get his feelings back under control and left for home. I silently hoped that if enough time would pass, he would get out of this cycle of want versus self-acceptance on his own. Unfortunately, I couldn't have been more wrong.

Weeks went on by like they had in the previous few months and I observed no change in the young man. He still did exactly as he had done before. He still sat there on the same bench, with the same heartbroken but stubborn expression and continued to sketch and now paint like his life depended on it.

Maybe it did.

"How are you today?" I asked, hoping my genuine concern would stir something within him.

"Fine." He said distractedly and continued focusing on his canvas.

I took a moment to really see him. It seemed like he'd lost a lot of weight. His cheeks had sunken in, his eyes were hollow and had bags underneath, and he seemed to have trouble breathing air in and out of his lungs; almost like he was close to wheezing with every breath he took.

"You don't really look fine," I whispered.

He whipped his head around to look at me almost as if accusing me of stating the truth out loud.

"*I said I'm fine!*" He spoke each word with as much venom as he could muster.

Instead of taking offence like anyone else would've, I chose to look beyond his anger. I knew immediately that this young man was, unfortunately, quite depressed.

"Okay, I understand. But maybe a little outside help wouldn't hurt." I said, hoping he wouldn't take offence at my suggestion. But he did.

"What do you mean?! I'm not crazy! I don't need a shrink!" He yelled and began packing up his things. I knew I didn't have a lot of time to convince him to seek help before he walked away from me.

I grabbed his shoulder and said, "Of course, you're not crazy! But it's okay to ask for a little help when you need it, you know?"

He angrily pushed my hand away. "I don't need a therapist. I'm not crazy!"

I knew if I said anything more in that moment, it wouldn't end well for either of us. So, I decided to let him go and cool off. It would probably be better if I approached this topic some other time anyway.

So, I sat back down on that bench and took out my diary; my true companion that housed all of my musings and learnings from these past years in hopes that I would eventually learn how to live a meaningful and satisfied life.

I wrote about the young man, about his troubles, his talent, and his wonderfully unrelenting love; even if that love was eating him up from the inside out. I pondered upon the need for self-acceptance, something that I rarely saw in anybody these days owing to the need to perfect our outsides (bodies) rather than fulling our insides (minds and souls).

If the young man had looked at his life from a different perspective, maybe given himself a lot more credit for his talent in painting, his love for music and movies, or if he'd seen himself as a whole human being, complete without really needing the love of the girl he was so madly in love with; maybe then, he'd realise he was worth so much more than the worth he'd assigned to himself. With all of his life experiences, he somehow seemed to have come to the conclusion that his short height was his only defining feature, at least the only one that mattered, and the lack of love from the girl he loved was the only thing he wanted from life. His refusal to accept himself as complete was what had probably let him down a path full of insecurities and eventually, depression.

And this happening was nowhere an attempt of me to find further faults in the young man. It was merely an observation regarding more than most of the young people I've seen around me so far. It was really a big shame that despite all the knowledge around us, seeking help from a therapist or someone equally qualified, especially for your mental health is still such a taboo in this society.

If people took care of their minds and souls just like they try and take care of every other physical organ in their bodies, maybe they would find it a bit less difficult to live a more satisfied life.

So, that's when I decided; that the next time I saw the young man, I would try my best to reason with him and try to make him see that just a little bit of help was all he needed to get back on track. I would at least try and make him see the things that should really be given importance in his life. Maybe a perspective change would do the trick. But even as I wrote it down in my diary, I knew it was easier said than done.

Unfortunately, some higher powers decided that I would never even get the chance to talk to him again. Wait...no. It wasn't any higher power. It was the young man himself who'd made the decision.

Just a week later, I was on my way to the gallery once again but stopped right in the middle of my tracks just outside its doors. The breath in my lungs refused to leave as my eyes rested upon the beautiful memorial set up on the park bench. In the centre was a picture of the young man I had befriended, his art next to his picture, and his biography next to it. Just like the artists within the gallery.

My heart stopped as the realisation hit. The young man had committed suicide. I had seen the signs earlier this week. I had suggested he go get some help. But in the end, there was nothing more I could've done. After all, the willingness to seek help is also rarely found in people these days. But I so wished he had.

A silent tear fell below my chin and I took a long look at a life that could've been saved and lived to the fullest had the concepts of self-acceptance, compensation and the right kind of love been drilled into the young man's brain. If his conservative thoughts about the benefits of therapy hadn't existed, he might've listened to me and sought help when he needed it.

I turned around, my heart still heavy, and walked away from the gallery for the very first time. That night I wrote in my diary how important it was to keep my mental health in prime condition so that I could accept myself completely and live my life to its fullest without falling prey to its tragedies.

CHAPTER FOUR

IT'S ALL ABOUT THE MONEY, MONEY, MONEY!

I was surrounded by tall buildings and expensive-smelling people. The glass on the windows were crystal clear, reflecting sunlight off into distances that showed nothing but even taller buildings.

I craned my neck to look up as high as I could and still couldn't see the end of the tower right in front of me. A certain sense of pride rose up in my chest unannounced, at everything my kind had been able to achieve in the past centuries. A smile graced my lips at the thought of the immense success of our species on this planet and I ignored the little nagging voice in my head that warned me about the consequences and the very steep price humankind *was* paying and *will keep* paying for generations for this very success, both in terms of their quality and kind of life, and in terms of the planet that housed it.

I took a few steps forward and entered the building in front of me. Even though I couldn't see its end against the sky, I very well could enter it and have a look at the rest of the world instead from quite a distance off the ground.

Immediately, I am hit with the smell of expensive coffee and other beverages. My eyes settle on the plethora of dishes served by one of the high-end restaurants inside the building on my right. On my left, there is a giant bookstore with a staircase within it, taking its customers upstairs to a seating area. There are screens on every wall, some small and some large, with some showing global news, and the majority of others reporting on the financial standing of the world markets with a special focus on India.

Of course, they have everything here, this place and the towers surrounding it are known to be the centre of India's economic markets and all its dealings. For a second, my mind traced back to the view I had laid my eyes on outside my taxi window on my way here. I had noticed multiple high-end luxury shops but the one that stood out the most was a car dealership with an extremely expensive Lamborghini visible through its transparent glass windows. Almost as if tempting each onlooker with the fact that any of the beautiful, expensive cars within the showroom could be theirs anytime they wished it.

A car showroom, beautiful restaurants, mall-like buildings with centralised air conditioning, a library with a world of knowledge, and the people with financial expertise from around the world. If there was anyone who wanted to be someone in this country, they would try and get their fates to hand them a ticket to right where I was standing. A satisfied sigh escaped my lips when I realised, this was it. I was one of the few people to have made it here. However, that little voice in my head said I was only here to work on a project and didn't necessarily belong with the people who hung out here like it was their backyard.

I walk further into the heart of the building only to be greeted by multiple lifts going up and down, carrying people that are either busy on their phones, or iPads, or are busy talking to each other in hued professional tones about the current financial state of the world. There were five lifts in total, all surrounding me like I was in the centre of a circle, all leading up to the highest floors in the building. They were on the move constantly, just like the people inside them.

A *ding* sounded on my left and I immediately realised it was one of the lifts that was being emptied out on the ground floor, and it was my ticket to the floor I needed to be on. I quickly walked my way to the lift and patiently waited as everyone got off. Then just as patiently waited for everyone to get on after I did. As soon as it was in motion, I turned around and looked to the other side of it. The elevator let the rider look at everything outside the building as it rode upwards. It was almost like a window to the other world. And I say other world because of the obvious differences between people within this building and the ones outside. If the people in here were used to expensive suits, strong coffees and even more expensive dinners and cars, the people outside were used to the same three pairs of jeans, trousers and shirts as they rode their ten-year-old scooters or bicycles to work every day. If the people in here were used to long lunches and nap time hours in the middle of their days, people out there were used to quick ten-minute breaks before they go back to their monotonous jobs that, more often than not, lead to insomnia.

It was quite jarring looking at it. I know for a fact that all of us belong to the same planet and yet, somehow, the two kinds of people might as well have been two completely different species; one obviously superior to the other. And the only factor that divided the two kinds was obviously, access to money. It was a wonder how comfortably some people could live while others, no matter how much hard work they engaged in, never seemed to be able to get out of an almost fateful like life sentence of poverty.

A few seconds later, the lift *dinged* again and I knew it was time for me to get off. I walked out to be greeted by the grandest of the reception areas I'd ever seen in my life. All décor was a mix of gold and white. Even the lights above my head cast a golden hue, the like of a beautiful sunset.

I walked up to the smiling lady and said, "Hi, I have an appointment with Mr. Rajesh today."

The lady swiftly checked my details against a database on her computer, gave me a visitor's pass and said, "Please take a seat in the waiting room right there and we'll have someone call for you as soon as Mr. Rajesh is ready to receive guests."

I smiled and nodded my head before walking off towards the waiting room she pointed out to me. The first thing I noticed when I entered the waiting room was the strong but wonderful smell of expensive coffee. I looked around to see more people in suits with more newspapers and iPads in their hands, completely engrossed in whatever they were supposed to be doing while waiting for someone. I walked straight up to the coffee counter and placed an expensive order for myself. After all, it wasn't every day that I got to partake in such indulgences and feel like I belonged in the same community as the people around me.

For today, I wasn't just a man. I was a *Somebody*.

I picked up my coffee minutes later and sat down on an empty sofa in the far corner. It didn't take me long to finish the sweet drink, but as soon as I did, my eyes landed again on the shop adjacent to the waiting room. I took a look at my watch and realised; it might take Mr. Rajesh a bit longer to invite me to his office so I might as well have a look around. I glanced at the iPads in the hands of the man next to me and made my decision. The shop adjacent to the waiting room was an Apple gallery with special discounts for those who can access this part of the building. Where else would I find a better deal on one of the most expensive phones.

I walked out of the waiting room and into the gallery and started looking around for a phone I had my heart set on ever since I'd seen the advertisement on TV.

"Just this once," I said as I reasoned with my conscience when it began to sow doubt in my mind about my actions for the day.

As soon as I found the model I was looking for, I asked one of the workers to get me a packed piece of the same and in seconds, I had walked toward the counter, paid for my new phone and walked out of the gallery feeling both happy and exhausted at having spent such a large amount in a day.

As I walked towards the waiting room again, my eyes dragged me to a large floor-to-ceiling window on my left and I found myself looking at the other species again.

It seemed like their struggle was never-ending. I mentally whacked myself in the head for saying '*their*' instead of '*our*,' almost like one day in this building had successfully transitioned me into the superior species with a tonne of money accessible in my bank account, just waiting to be spent.

But the truth was far from it and my guilty conscience was very well aware of it. However, I tried my best to ignore that whiny voice in my head that asked me to realise my place in the world and not indulge in expenses that I would most certainly regret later in life.

I sat down in the waiting room again and, this time struck up a conversation with a younger-looking man beside me. He was reading a magazine about the newest model of cars and caught me looking at the very same beautiful Lamborghini on the front cover that I had seen through the dealership window on my way here. He gushed about its beauty just like I would've.

"It's the best one I've seen out of the company so far. Honestly, I think I might just go ahead and buy one soon." He said and squinted his eyes almost as if trying to remember something before continuing, "I think I saw one this morning at a car dealership. I'm pretty sure that's the only one left."

The smile vanished off my face and my heart began thumping loudly in my chest.

The only one left!

I immediately excused myself and stood up to walk out of the waiting room again. It was now or never. I took out my new phone and dialled the dealership's number after searching for it on the internet. In the next few minutes, I think I forgot to catch my breath because I had made the biggest expense of my life and transferred everything I had in my bank account to the dealership and made that beautiful Lamborghini, completely and only; MINE!

I took a deep breath and let it out. I did that a few more times until I managed to get my heart to beat a little less like a drum in my chest.

"What did I just do? I'm a middle-class man!" I thought to myself.

"I brought a Lamborghini for myself, is what I did! *I own a Lamborghini!*" I responded to myself. I'm quite sure I must've looked like a lunatic to the passersby. It didn't matter though. I now own one of the most expensive cars in the world! Talk about belonging to the superior species!

I walked back into the waiting room only to see the young man on a call with the same dealership. The frown on his face told me everything I needed to know. I had a hard time keeping the slight smile off my face for the rest of the wait time.

Soon, I was escorted into Mr. Rajesh's office and within an hour, was done with what I had come to this building for. Overall, I had a feeling that I had an extremely satisfactory day.

I walked out of the building with a bounce in my step like owned the ground I put my foot on. This happiness was unparalleled by anything I had ever felt before. It was like I was on cloud nine!

I hailed a taxi, promising myself to sign any papers that needed to be signed and to pick up that beautiful car first thing the next morning as the dealership was about to close soon.

As I sat in the back of the taxi, took out my brand-new phone and checked out my bank app, fully expecting the numbers I saw in it, or rather, the lack of. I knew in the back of my mind that I had blown away every single penny I'd saved in the past ten years today on this new phone and the new car. No, wait, I had blown it all away to belong to the higher class for just a little longer. Or at least, pretend to belong to one.

But none of that reasoning that I so wanted to see as logical shadowed the fact that I had just emptied my bank account and had no access to a safety net for me or my family anymore in case of some emergency. I had no insurance and nothing saved up in case something happened to me or any of my family members. I was down to living paycheck by paycheck.

It did occur to me that because of my need to pretend to belong to the higher class of people, I had ultimately reduced myself in terms of monetary access to the class of people I so desperately wanted to get away from. It had been a day of stupid decisions, I knew that very well. But stubbornly, I refused to dwell on it just yet.

But the second I switched off the screen of my new phone and placed it into the side pocket of my pants, the whole world seemed to slow down. Saw a larger car than ours racing towards us at full speed. My brain knew what was happening moments before it happened.

Even though the crash was sudden and the breath in my lungs was knocked out and my head was cracked open seconds later, I was conscious enough to know I was going to die.

That's when the panic began to set in.

Not when I knew the car was going to crash into us; or when it finally did crash into us; the panic set in when I realised, I was going to die. But the panic wasn't for my death. It was for the fact that my actions today had sealed my family's fate and left them without any safety net to fall back on after I was gone. My greed had not only cost me, but also them, everything.

With my last few breaths, all I could ask god was a do-over so that instead of spending all that money on phones and cars and coffees; on things that don't really matter, I could get insurance for each member of my family and invest whatever was leftover into things that would ensure long term financial gain.

But that was all I could do at the end; pray.

I opened my eyes and found myself on my bed. My shirt was soaked through with sweat and my heart beat in my chest like a drum. *I was alive!*

Immediately the realisation set in that this was all a nightmare. Regardless, I had learned my lesson and fortunately, I think this was the do-over my prayers got me. So, I immediately sat up and got out of bed to do exactly what I had promised myself if I had another chance.

CHAPTER FIVE

TO BE A GROUNDED TREE

It was a bright summer day when I finally made the decision to take a little break from working. I had been working continuously for almost two decades now and sure, I'd learned a lot about work and life along the way. But now, I had just reached a point where I wanted to do nothing but sit by myself at home and wonder about the life I've lived so far and the life I was yet to live.

So, I did just that. I handed in my notice a month ago, and now, I had all the time in the world to do exactly as I liked; which, at the moment, was doing nothing. I got out of bed, made myself some tea and walked out the backdoor to look at the beautiful backyard my sister made sure to always keep almost absolutely immaculate.

There it was, the massive tree that had accompanied me, and often enough accompanied my sister, in our lives from the first day that I bought this house. The day was as vivid in my mind as the sun was in my eyes right then. I had signed the deed for the house a day before she was supposed to get married and move out of our parents' house. She had come home straight to the new house after having attended all the festivities and we were finally able to catch our breaths. It felt like forever that we'd had a chance to just sit and relax in each other's company ever since I had moved out on my own. So that night, we'd decided to revel in the silence, look at each other and just smile as we tried not to think too deeply about the new stages of life we were both going to enter into pretty soon.

After an hour of doing the same and talking about everything and nothing at all, my sister had suddenly got up and walked over to her bag that she carried with her all the time but had now discarded in one corner of the house. She'd opened the topmost zipper and pulled out a bag of seeds from within it. She'd gently tapped on my shoulder and smiled at me before leading me to our backyard. She'd almost immediately found a shovel soon after, and before I knew it, I was digging a small hole in the ground with the biggest smile on my face.

"This is going to be our beacon. The thing we come home to that reminds us of how we came to be. When our parents see it standing proud and tall in your backyard, remind them of the fact that they made us just to be like that tree; with all the world's strength and with roots that go deeper than just familial bond," she'd said with a big smile on her face as she dumped the seeds in the hole I'd just dug and immediately covered it up with dirt. And just like that, she'd immediately taken up the responsibility of keeping my backyard at its best always.

I still remember how I had felt like a little kid that day, looking up at my sister as she told me that we were going to live a good life and that the tree was going to be the proof of the same. Slowly but steadily, the familial love and that tree made the house my forever home. And before I knew it, this tree had taken root in my garden and was as much a part of our family as me and my sister were.

I quietly sat under the tree's shade and let my mind wander. I wondered what would've occurred had this tree been given less than what it had received so far in all of these years it has been a part of our family. What if there had been less sunlight, or either of us had forgotten to water it, or forgotten to take care of the reckless weeds growing in our backyard that could potentially harm it? What if we'd neglected this tree, intentionally or otherwise? Would it have still grown to be such a beauty and a beacon of our lives?

Before I could answer my own questions, my phone alerted me of a text I'd received right then. It was from a college friend of mine I'd kept in touch with since.

"Just wanted to let you know that Nikhil got into that Ivy League university we talked about the last time we spoke!"

My heart swelled with pride as I recalled my friend's son. I immediately appreciated everything my friend and his wife had done for Nikhil. To get him to this position was not just to credit Nikhil's efforts but also that of his parents. After all, Nikhil wasn't exactly like the other boys of his age.

I still remember that day almost two decades ago. It had been a hot summer day when I'd received a call from my friend. He'd been completely ecstatic to deliver the news that finally, after nine months of what seemed like a non-stop struggle of pregnancy on behalf of his wife, they'd finally been blessed with twin boys.

"Congratulations!" I'd immediately yelled into the phone and rushed out to meet them at their home. Two beautiful baby boys had welcomed me only hours after the call.

My friends did a great job of making the task of raising two boys on their own look easy. Especially after the initial diagnosis was handed to them. A couple of years after the boys' birth, the couple had found themselves in the doctor's office waiting to hear the result of the multiple tests done on their boys to gauge whether their mental capacity was average for boys of their age.

The doctor's hesitation at the time had said volumes before he even had to open his mouth.

"Raj is doing great for his age according to the tests but Nikhil just isn't catching up, I'm afraid." The doctor had said to the couple in the calmest tone he could muster. But even that calm couldn't have stopped the storm raging in a parent's mind as they heard the news that their child was most probably not going to have a normal life; that he would almost always need extra attention, and maybe even then, he could still fail to catch up to his peers.

At first, the couple behaved almost as though the doctor was mental and had most certainly misdiagnosed their child. But soon enough, there were signs to confirm the doctor's interpretation of results and they could not ignore the matter any longer. Then came the anger; and they would ask, sometimes quietly in despair and sometimes loudly with distaste, at whatever god was present that how could he do that to them.

After a while, when the storm of emotions was no longer a surprise, and the slow mental growth of their child became a footnote of their life, they finally decided to tackle it head-on.

They figured out the areas where their child lacked the mental capacity to grow along with his peers. But in that phrasing of words, they realised, he didn't exactly lack the mental capacity to grow at all, just to grow at the speed that his peers did. This meant that if they could just put in enough effort, they would be able to bring him up to their level for sure.

They began by building a library in their home and filled it with every book they could imagine would help their child grow up to match the intellectual capacity with that of the kids around him. They spent every night reading to him in bed. They spent hours and hours every day, researching and figuring out games, exercises, counsellors, and tutors that would help him reach his full intellectual capacity. They changed his diet after consulting multiple nutritionists to make it so that he had the best nutritional supply they could afford and that all his elevated energy would be focused on one thing and one thing alone; to catch up to everyone else; to be the boy that isn't ever left behind.

They spent what remaining hours of the day they could find free, after committing to all of the above and working at their jobs, playing with him to make sure he never felt overwhelmed or unloved.

All in all, they did their best as parents to make sure that their kid was never at a disadvantage if they could help it. And unsurprisingly, their efforts brought in wonderous results. Nikhil took a few years, but he caught up to the smartest kid in his class. Slowly but steadily, he proved to be a well-developed and well-rounded child at school. He was kind, knew when to focus, knew when to take a break and always had a smile on his face no matter what obstacle was thrown his way. The years and hours and efforts his parents had spent on teaching him and grooming him had resulted in a very intellectually enlightened child who would never again be known as the one falling behind his peers.

His parents had seen the constant growth in their child and decided to aim just a little higher after his high school graduation. They decided to apply to one of the biggest Ivy League schools in the country in the hopes that the tradition of their son receiving the most attention and the very best of education would continue even after they'd done their part.

And as expected of their brilliant child, Nikhil did get into the school and even earned a merit-based scholarship which lessened the financial load on his parents.

And as I received this news today, sitting in the backyard, pondering upon life under the shade of our family tree, I couldn't help but feel just as proud of the child as his parents do. Even if I had always been on the sidelines, looking at the child's and his parent's efforts at making him the best version of himself, I couldn't help but feel happiness swelling in my chest at the thought of Nikhil in the graduation cap he would receive a few years later which would make a straight path for him to walk towards a successful future; or at least a financially stable one.

It made me think about the tree again. Just like the tree over these wonderful years, Nikhil had successfully received enough intellectual encouragement from his parents and was now almost like a strong tree himself, ready to set his roots down and become a beacon for his family.

Just then, my eyes travelled to a smaller sapling hidden behind the larger tree in my backyard. It was so well covered by the tree trunk that I wouldn't have noticed it in a million years had I not sat down right next to the big trunk.

The plant seemed to be the same kind as the tree and only seemed to be a few months to a year old at best. But it was already so much different than the tree itself. Where the tree had its bright leaves and strong branches and a bunch of flowers which were eventually going to turn into delicious fruit; this plant looked dried up, with leaves falling faster than they grew, with thin enough twigs that even a little child could break them with little to no effort; it looked like it was just about ready to die.

Just as I was about to approach that little plant, my phone notified me of another text message. I stopped in my path and read it: "Hi Uncle, It's me, Raj. You must've heard that Nikhil got into that university everyone had been talking about for the past year. I had applied too. And I didn't get in. I didn't want to tell my parents and let them be disappointed in me. Again. So, I thought of reaching out to you instead."

My heart sank down to my stomach as I read the text and realised what a massive thing all of us adults had missed out on while we were all so focused on Nikhil and his future.

While Nikhil was watered and fed and encouraged to grow every second of his life until he could become something akin to a grounded tree; Raj, just for already being of average intellect, had been completely ignored under the assumption that the child would grow up fine on his own, and had turned out to be like the sad little withered sapling in my backyard.

I wondered for a moment whether the fault lay with his parents. That in trying to make sure that one of their children would never become a failure, they ultimately ended up doing that for their other child. Suddenly, looking at the big tree, the sapling next to it and the text messages from both Nikhil's father and Raj himself made me realise just how important it is to take care of, feed, and foster intellectual health in a human being. And just because someone already seems of a certain IQ, it doesn't mean that their learning should ever end there. The growth of intellect is always an ongoing process. It will never have an end as long as there are knowledgeable resources on the planet. There will always be something more to learn and someone better to be.

I took one last look at the plant life in my backyard, stood up and texted Raj, "Would you like to come over for some tea, son?"

Even if it was late, I decided I was now going to step up and help Raj out where he needed it; provide the attention and the efforts that he sadly missed out on in his childhood. After all, just like the growth of intellect can never end in someone, it is also never too late to begin fostering it.

CHAPTER SIX

WHO WILL GIVE ME A KIDNEY?

Once again, I walked into a room where nothing but the beeping monitors made any sound. However, this time I was here to take an interview of a semi-healthy person and not to sit by a friend's bed, praying and hoping that they would wake up from their traumatic injuries soon.

As soon as I entered the room, Mr. Dhruv looked at me from the bed and smiled before making much effort to sit up on the hospital bed.

"I'm sorry, all of these tubes sticking out of me make it so much harder to move." He said as he gently put his legs on the ground, clutched the mobile part of the machines and walked toward the table in the corner of the room.

"I can only imagine. Thank you for agreeing to be interviewed at such a time in your life. I'm sure a lot of people are curious as to how you're holding up." I motioned toward the seat opposite him, asking whether it was okay for me to sit down.

"Yes, of course! Please take a seat." Mr. Dhruv smiled painfully and continued, "I'm sure everyone's curious enough. So, let's get this done, shall we?"

I took the hint immediately and started firing question after question. After all, the article I would write about this interview was definitely going to be the most searched one at least for a month due to just how famous Mr. Dhruv was both in the country and internationally.

I chose to begin at the beginning. "I know the fame is something that you've now become quite accustomed to, but were you in a similar position throughout your life or was it something specific that made you choose the limelight as soon as you hit twenty?"

Mr. Dhruv gave a light chuckle at my question and looked as if he was remembering a distant, yet, very nostalgic past in order to give an accurate answer.

"I had always been popular. At least, as far as I can remember. I know, it might sound extremely arrogant but it's the truth. I don't remember too many specifics from my time in high school but what I do remember is that I was never short of friends. Or admirers. Call them what you may. It doesn't matter."

I opened my work notebook and started jotting down some points to help me remember Mr. Dhruv's answers as accurately as I could. I nodded along to his speech, silently encouraging him to keep talking and to keep giving me as much information as he could.

"I mean, you must remember how it was to be seventeen. All the vanity and none of the sincerity. Our bodies were always appreciated but never for the right reasons. We always found something to chase, whether it be beauty or popularity." Mr. Dhruv crossed his hands and took a pause as he looked down at his boots. It looked like he had lost his train of thought.

I clicked the back of my pen once hoping to bring his mind back into this room from wherever it had wandered but it did no good. So, I asked another question, "And you had both, didn't you? I mean you had the looks and the popularity?"

"Yes, I had both. And I was chased around by many for both. In high school and even much later in my life."

Mr. Dhruv didn't seem to want to elaborate any further on the topic so I decided to let it go and ask a different leading question. This chase of beauty and popularity really didn't tell me much about the kind of man he was or the kind of life he had led so far anyway.

"Is there anything memorable about your high school days? Something other than your obvious popularity?" I crossed my legs and leaned back into the chair I was sitting on hoping this would turn out to be a longer conversation than I was expecting. After all, it isn't every day you get to interview and write about a national heartthrob sitting right in front of you.

A genuine laugh tore out of Mr. Dhruv's lips this time, surprising both me and him by the looks of it. But the memory soon filled his eyes as he began speaking. "Yes. Yes, there's definitely one day I remember extremely vividly. A day I don't think I will ever forget in my entire life. Especially considering my situation now."

I stayed quiet, hoping my silence was enough encouragement, and Mr. Dhruv did not disappoint.

"There was nothing out of the ordinary about how that day began, to be honest. I was surrounded by my classmates, girls from the neighbouring school," Mr. Dhruv winked at me knowingly before continuing, "Anyway. It was lunchtime and for some reason I had this urge to get myself alone somehow and be silent. I must've been quite overwhelmed. So, I did. I shooed everyone away, which was just as difficult back then as it is today, and made my way up to the rooftop. I remember thinking how lucky I was that no one seemed to be on the rooftop and the fact that I had it to myself was a miracle on its own. It was an open space, seven floors up, sort of square in shape, and surrounded by thick white walls that came to my shoulders when I leaned on them. A few minutes into the silence, I heard footsteps. My first thought was to go hide somewhere but before I could have even moved, I spotted him. Justin. He was only a year younger than I was. And yet, he seemed much smaller physically. He had been lying on the floor, not moving, not making a sound, all the while I had been there. And one look at his face told me why. He had so many bruises on him. In fact, if it hadn't been for his nametag, I don't think I would've recognized him at all that day. His eyes were almost swollen shut, there was so much bruising on his cheeks, his lips were bleeding and his teeth were stained red. He seemed to be wheezing with every breath he took and the limp in his leg was definitely more than a sprain at first glance." Mr. Dhruv looked at me sheepishly and said, "I know, I know. Too graphic."

"No! No! I would really like to know exactly what happened. Paint me a picture."

When Mr. Dhruv bit his lips, unsure whether he should continue with the story, I piped up again, "So…What happened to Justin?"

Mr. Dhruv sighed and continued, "Well…It was obvious. It looked like he'd been beaten up pretty bad. But before I could call out to him and ask if he was okay—which he obviously wasn't—he climbed up on one of the walls of the rooftop. I remember my heart feeling like it had dropped to my stomach. So, I had called out to him before he could take another step. I guess the desperation in my voice was clear enough to make him stop in his tracks. I had asked him his name in hopes of getting him talking, but he had stayed silent. I think it was about five minutes of him not speaking at all, just standing on the ledge looking at me stuttering and trying to find the right words to get him to step down. I remember it feeling like it was the longest five minutes of my life.

"Anyway, the first words out of his mouth back then were, '*Why do I even need to continue?*' And just like that, he was crying, and trying not to wheeze at the same time. I don't really remember much about what happened after; only that I had sat next to him till the sun had set and the security guard had come up to lock the rooftop door and found us there. Turns out, he was being bullied because he belonged to a different caste than the majority of the student population at the school. And the fact that his parents didn't have much to their name didn't help much either. He didn't have any friends and the bullying had been going on for a few years now. And judging by his face, for whatever reason, it had turned quite violent. And I don't know what came over me that day, but I promised myself to help this kid in any way I could. And I did." Mr. Dhruv's smile this time was encased in elation. "I went to school the next day, found the kids that had done that to Justin and basically made them social outcasts. I made sure to stick next to Justin for the rest of our high school days. I made sure he was okay. Those were probably the best days of my life back then. Nothing could compare to the satisfaction I'd felt when I'd finally seen Justin's face without any bruises and looked at his lips curling up into a smile. I dare say all this fame and popularity till this day doesn't even come close to that feeling."

I jotted down points into my notebook religiously before asking him to confirm, "You saved his life. Nothing compares to that feeling of success, does it?"

"No. No, it doesn't. But it wasn't success that I was feeling. I think it was just pure relief at averting a tragedy, even if the tragedy wasn't mine. Anyway, since then. It was all uphill. As soon as I graduated high school, I was flooded with so many modelling and advertising contracts. Mind you, I didn't know a thing about modelling or acting back then. But it didn't matter. I had the face people would want to see on screen. And that's it, I just followed fate and reached where I am today."

I nodded and suddenly another question jumped up in my head. I took out my phone, searched for Mr. Dhruv's Instagram profile and felt my eyebrows shoot up in shock. "Wow! Forty-eight million followers! How does all of this fame make you feel? Are you now used to every eye turning towards you when you walk through a door?"

Mr. Dhruv folded his arms and crossed his legs, adjusting himself into a more comfortable posture. It looked to me as if he was trying to find a way to answer this and not offend millions out there. I gave him his time and he finally spoke up, "It has definitely made me feel like I'm on the top of the world most of the time. I came from a lower middle-class background but now I have free entry to places only the top one percent of the country gets to walk into. But nothing made me realise my power, or rather the power of my fame, until social media came around. I mean, this one time I'd posted on Instagram about this underrated and undiscovered restaurant that I had loved dining at and if you look at them now, they've opened 5 branches around the country and there's always a minimum of a month's waiting list to get into any of them for even a single evening. I realised then that I could literally make or break a business and to an extreme…people as well. It's a whirlwind for sure, this fame game."

I pressed my lips together, finally understanding what he was trying to say, "It's bittersweet."

"Yes, yes, it is."

"May I ask what exactly happened that you landed in a hospital? I mean, I've seen the stories on Instagram and some news headlines but I thought it'd be better to hear it from the man himself."

Mr. Dhruv took a deep breath and then let it out. All the poise from his posture suddenly vanished and it almost felt like this was the most candid version of him anyone would ever have access to.

"I was diagnosed with acute renal failure a few weeks ago and had to be put on dialysis soon after. That's what my Instagram stories were all about. I needed a kidney. I needed *someone to give me a kidney*."

"It must've worked, right? Considering you're here for your transplant today?"

"Yes, I'm here for my transplant today but begging on social media didn't work at all. In fact, all it did was open my eyes to just how alone I was in this real world where fame doesn't rule it all."

Before I could ask further to clarify my confusion, the door on my right opened and a doctor walked in, greeting Mr. Dhruv first and then taking a chair from the other corner of the room and sitting down with us.

Mr. Dhruv smiled at the doctor sitting down and introduced him, "Meet the man who's saving my life today."

I immediately put my palm out for a handshake and thanked him on behalf of the entire nation for saving this heartthrob's life by performing this very important surgery.

The doctor laughed and said, "No, no, I think you've got it wrong. I'm not the surgeon. I'm the kidney donor. It's nice to meet you. I'm Justin"

The doctor shook my hand and immediately the pieces began to click in my head. The doctor was the donor and not the surgeon. And he was called Justin. Probably the same Justin that Mr. Dhruv saved all those years ago.

Mr. Dhruv looked at my face and confirmed my thoughts with a smile. "You see, I was hoping that out of the hordes of followers I had on every social media account possible, at least one person would come up and get tested to see if were a match and save my life. But I realised it soon enough. It was all an illusion. This digital life that we all carry in our back pockets and hang onto it like our lifeline, it's all a hoax. No one will come out to help you when you really need it. At least, none of your so-called digital friends. You know, when I initially began posting about my renal failure, I was under the impression that I would find a donor almost immediately. But I soon realised that all the sympathy I received would only remain behind phone screens and never translate into actual actions. I realised I was actually completely alone.

"But then, coincidently, I met Justin again in this hospital after, gosh, how long has it been? Almost eighteen years, right? Yeah, for the first time after eighteen years. And you know, the second he found out about my problem, the first words out of his mouth were, '*Let me get tested to see if I'm a match.*' You have no idea how thankful I was for that."

Justin chuckled, turned to Mr. Dhruv and said, "Of course. This is just me paying back the kindness I'd received from you back then. I wouldn't be here if it wasn't for you. You literally saved my life that day. I'm just glad I get to save yours now."

I looked at Mr. Dhruv and noticed the tears in his eyes. This was a friendship worth writing about and a lesson worth learning about. People need to wake up and really live in the world around them instead of just existing digitally, because when the real moments in life come around, it's not the digital relationships you rely on for support and help, it's the real-life friendships that help you get through it all. Mr. Dhruv's story was a lesson that this generation sorely needed to learn.

I looked at the book in my hand and figured, I had enough material to write that article now so I took my leave and pondered on the title for the same. As soon as I left the hospital, it came to me. I grinned and wrote the sentence in my notebook so that I wouldn't forget it as I walked out of the hospital. The title I settled on was: "WHO WILL GIVE ME A KIDNEY?"

THE TORNADO WITHIN

The doorbell rang. I got up from the couch to walk towards my door and open it. I had already seen Raj's car park itself down the street a few minutes ago so I knew it couldn't be anyone but him. As soon as I had the door open though, he flew straight into my arms, hugging me tightly, almost as if I could somehow make the world around him disappear if I hugged him just a little stronger. That was all I really needed to know about how my friend's other twin was doing. Just a few days ago, I'd been sitting in the backyard thinking of Nikhil, the brother who had gotten into an Ivy League school in spite of the doctors telling his parents at birth that he had no chance at a successful life. And now, when all the celebrations of that event had died down, I could see just how much it was bothering Raj in front of me.

"Come in, son!" I said with a big, bright smile; unsure of how I should bring my notice of his feelings up. But I realised soon enough that I didn't have to make that effort at all. As soon as I had that warm cup of tea set in front of him, he took one look at my face and broke down completely into heart-wrenching sobs and tears. I let him cry; let him get it out as much as I could before I decided to say something about it all.

"I'm fairly certain I have an idea about what it is that is making you so very sad. But can you tell me what's going on anyway?" I nudged Raj to open up to me.

After allowing a few seconds for his hiccups to settle down, the young man wiped his eyes, looked at me and said, "I'm not sad at all, uncle. In fact, all I am feeling right now is frustrated. And very, very angry."

"Angry?" I waited for him to elaborate. But when he didn't, I took matters into my own hands. "Okay. Anger it is. Get up, come on." I reached a hand out toward the young man on the couch and he looked up at me with a questioning eye.

"Just trust me, okay?" I said again and he finally took my hand. Minutes later, he was sat in the passenger seat of my car, safety belt all buckled in as I drove us out of the gated community that I liked to call home.

"Where are we going, uncle?" Raj sniffled a little. His hiccups had died down a few minutes ago and now he was distractedly looking out of the window, trying to figure out our final destination.

"You'll see when we get there. All I can tell you right now is, if you're feeling all this anger that has no other choice but to express itself as frustration and tears, the place we're going to is definitely going to help you deal with all that overflow."

After that, Raj stayed quiet, lost in thought but no less fidgety from the anticipation. As soon as we arrived though, he let out a deep breath, almost like he had been holding it for quite a while now and chuckled. "Why did I not think of going into a rage room before?!"

"Because only after talking to me did you realise it was anger at all that you needed to deal with." I smiled at him as I parked the car in the giant but empty parking lot, considering it was in the middle of the afternoon right now.

"Let's go." We were in the wide building in seconds and the employees had suited us and put a helmet on our heads before handing us both a steel bat and locking us in into one of the ugly graffitied rooms filled with things to break.

"This is nice." Raj looked around trying to decide what he should go after first. Immediately, his eyes landed on the glass bottles in the far corner of the room. He looked back at me almost as if to ask permission first. I nodded and he immediately jogged over and picked up the bottles one by one, smashing them onto the floor and the walls in front of him with as much force as he could.

When no more bottles remained, he looked around for something else. There was a mirror hanging on the wall beside me, far enough away that I couldn't get hurt. He made a beeline for it and before I could react, the steel bat in his hands was through the glass and the wooden frame that held it together was broken and splintered on the floor alongside the shattered mess.

This went on for a little more than an hour. We had gone into the room with Raj feeling a lot of rage and anger within him and had come out with his head being a lot lighter and the room completely destroyed. Raj's shoulders were less taught, his jaw unclenched and his hands were back in his pockets like he was pretending to be all cool for the people around him. All in all, he was feeling better.

As soon as he got home with me though, he asked for more tea. But before I even set his cup down on the table, his eyes were once again filled with tears.

"Anger, we have dealt with," I said as I sat down opposite him. "What are you feeling now?"

His hiccups were back as he visibly tried to put his feelings into words. "When I was seven, we had a play in school. Both Nikhil and

I had auditioned for the lead. When Nikhil said the lines flawlessly, he was made the lead. I had said them flawlessly too, but I was made the understudy. I had been so mad that day. I'd gone up to the teacher and asked her: why Nikhil and not me? She had just simply said, what if he never gets a better chance? I should learn to open up paths for my brother instead of coveting them for myself. And from then on, that was all I had ever tried to do. Helped him finish his homework first even though I had to spend more hours trying to do mine. Which, I failed at sometimes and lost a grade because of it. I helped him get friends and was as supportive as I could've been. And I know what I'm about to say is extremely selfish of me, but I feel like Nikhil is living the life I was supposed to. In fact, I would've lived it had I not made efforts at being the second best my entire life so that my brother who was at a major disadvantage would get the best out of his life."

I waited for a few more seconds as he gathered himself and wiped the tears off his cheeks.

He took a deep breath and said, "I guess I'm trying to tell you I'm extremely sad that I'm such a failure. And I hate that I'm trying to find a way to blame my amazing brother for that; or even my parents, who always, always put him first for everything."

I folded my arms trying to think of a way to say it correctly. "Your parents were trying to help him with his intellectual capacity. I know that that must've led to some neglect for you, but you didn't need as much help as your brother did. As for what you're feeling right now; it's an extremely emotional reaction to the situation. Now, I can't help you much with the former but I definitely can help you figure out how to take care of your emotions and yourself as you learn to suffer through them. Because unlike intellectual health, which was your parents' responsibility, emotional health is something only you can manage for yourself."

"Do you mean my mental health?" Raj sat up straight now, wholly willing to give this discussion a chance and find his way through the tornado within.

"Not exactly. Mental health is more like an umbrella term that includes aspects of emotional health. If I had to explain it to you in layman's terms, I'd say emotional health is all about how well you recognize and manage your emotions." I took a sip of my tea and urged Raj to ask more questions if he wanted to.

"And how do we do that?" Raj asked, his brows furrowed in confusion.

"We need to first understand just how complex human emotions are. The fact that sadness does not necessarily mean depression, or that feeling insecure can sometimes be mistaken as fear or anxiety instead of the latter two being a result of the insecurity, it is all quite difficult for most adults to differentiate, recognize and accept. Truth be told, sometimes even I mess them up to this date. And obviously, there are so many more emotions that we have to deal with every single day of our lives. So, as I said before, it's a process that takes practice to master. However, it is important that you don't mistake managing emotions for controlling them. Managing will let you feel what you need to feel and as you work through it towards calm and peace, controlling might just mean you bury it, and in the long run, it's worse for your overall mental health. Like, if anger is an emotion which is bothering you, then it is important to understand the reason for the anger and see how we behave in that situation initially and what the consequences would be for the same. I know it may all sound very overwhelming right now but trust me when I tell you, you've already begun to figure the process out for yourself."

When Raj's confusion increased at my last statement, I clarified, "You already recognised by yourself that you needed some help. You reached out to me for the same. So, you see, you've already taken the first step in learning how to manage your emotions. Then, when you finally said out loud that it wasn't sadness at all that you were feeling, but anger, I took you to the rage room. This provided a safe environment for you to realise your feelings without the risk of damaging anyone else, including you, either physically or mentally. Most people don't realise that they need help adjusting to the emotional turmoil within so they never reach out to friends or professionals. Professionals can usually help in setting up processes in your mind so that eventually, the tornado of emotions that is bound to rise now and then just feels like a heavy breeze to be weathered."

Raj remained quiet for a few seconds and then asked, "Will I always need a rage room to vent my anger? Or a close family friend to help me get through my sadness and frustration?"

I smiled. "No. Not always. You still may need it all sometimes; we are all humans, after all. But no, not always."

"Will I ever figure it all out?"

"You will. It'll take time. But you will. Remember what I've said multiple times today; maintaining emotional health is a continuous process."

Raj nodded in understanding. "How will I know if I'd finally achieved a good standing with my emotional health."

I took out my phone and texted him the 7-step checklist that I used to gauge my emotional health all these years.

He immediately took his phone out and read it.

7 Signs of Emotional Wellness:

1. *You are comfortable with who you are.*
2. *You are adaptable and resilient.*
3. *You have positive relationships with the people in your life.*
4. *You have a sense of purpose.*
5. *You take care of your physical health.*
6. *You are comfortable saying 'no.'*
7. *You make time to relax.*

"Sounds like a solid checklist," Raj said and smiled at me. This time, his smile reached his eyes.

Relief flooded my veins as the minutes went by. The tea was cold and the sun had begun to set by the time we ended our day. Raj left that day with a lighter heart, and mine swelled with pride for the kind of man he was growing up to be: A man who recognizes where he lacks and isn't afraid to ask for help.

Access: Restricted

Aspects like wealth creation would happen once we are able to identify & develop skills which can be monetised and this is perfectly in our own hands.

Health has 3 aspects viz., Physical, Mental & Emotional. Health contains something natural called as self-healing process, Control mechanisms, multiple specialists available to address health related issues.

But amongst all the six aspects covered in detail so far, one of the most important and critical aspect which is more external than being internal is the social relationship.

We need to be extra cautious to understand who we are allowing into our circle and we need to be very careful in deciding up to what extent we are going to give access to them into our circle.

It is very important to understand that once we have given certain access to outsiders, they might not want to move away or give it up, even if we wish & there are so many relationships which will have a legal tangle attached to it. Hence, be cautious while developing your Relationship circle but at the same time don't hesitate to give up relationships if it becomes toxic. But if you are very serious about certain about certain relationships, don't forget to Respect it, Care for it and Support the person in the Relationship.

"Relationships can make you or Break you"

Pictorial Representation Of 3 Key Aspects To Live A Happy Life:

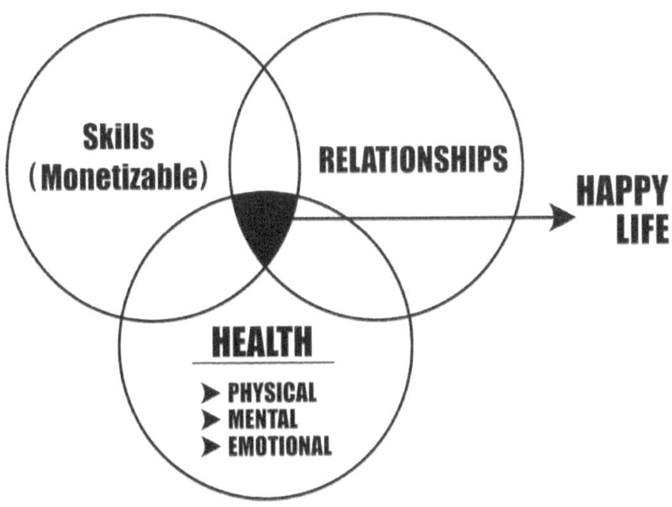

Dear Reader

It is with great pleasure and an equitable sadness, that I pen this letter to you. Pleasure—for the fact that you have made it to the end of this book and have taken in the learnings I wanted to give out; Sadness—for the fact that you have made it to the end of this book and we must now bid a regretful goodbye.

That's right; it was a goodbye that initially motivated me to write about the concepts of life and death and their many interpretations. I have tried, now and again, to explore what it all could mean to people who are still learning the ropes of life. I have tried to pry out of the invisible hands of the universe, the secret to successful living, like so many have done before me. And it is a bittersweet feeling being able to share these findings with you, knowing they may not fit you like a glove, for you are surely different than I am, but realising and taking comfort in the fact that they just may guide you to some truth moulded only for you.

It is a strange and repetitive concept this death. And it is surprisingly always on time. It may not be a convenient time for you, but it arrives exactly when it's supposed to. At least in my ancestors' case, more often than not, it seemed like that clock always stopped ticking around fifty years of age. Strange, I know; but true. It was true for my grandfather, who died at fifty, and for my father, who followed the same fate when he turned that age. And it was true for men in my family who were born well before my grandfather as well. Now, some may label it as mere coincidence, but for someone who thinks he may very well be beholden to a similar fate, death is a matter that needs to be explored.

Let me elaborate. I am, for the sake of your understanding, a forty-eight-year-old man. I am just two years shy of when my father and his father both faced their ends. Hence, it is ultimately natural that my head turned towards thoughts of death, and in turn, turned towards thoughts of how well I've lived my life and succeeded at being satisfied with whatever I've had in my life so far.

I have met many people, forgotten most, maintained my relationship with some, and just like the fates of my father and his father, I've seen others who have faced a similar tragic fate. I will not claim that my learnings are all that you need in life to feel like you've made it and would be satisfied if death was to come for you next. But I hope that they will at least set you on the right path to the discovery of the same, for I do acknowledge that the truth and its discovery isn't usually made by always walking on the same path. I hope that you learn what you need to in order to go through life as smoothly as rowing through still seas and not face the raging storms with zero understanding of how to successfully sail through them. Yes, that is exactly what I look at life like; it's a boat handed to you at the beginning of your journey. The size or the make of it isn't ever under your control. But your skills with sailing it will ensure your survival through the worst of the thunderstorms.

There is one more thing along with your skills and learnings of how to weather storms regardless of where they are (in your life or out at sea) that ensures you do become the best version of yourself. I have already given you the tools to achieve exactly that in this book but there is a quality you must develop within you alongside it all; resilience.

It is simply a fact of life that you will fail. Whatever it is that you choose to do, you are bound to fail at least once or twice. It is very rare to succeed at something difficult the very first time you try it. So, in the end, all I can do is to urge you to always be resilient in your efforts to live the best possible life you can.

If you are into parenting, teach your kids about some of the things which we have discussed in this book from a very young age so that they live a life which is far more satisfying.

Like all the motivational speakers, trainers and philosophers tell us, we can reach a destination only if we know it. Fortunately or unfortunately, we all know our final destination which happens to be "DEATH" and there is nothing wrong in planning for this one FINAL Destination.

"Live Well"

to

"Die Happily"